My Faith Journal
thoughts and musings

Journal of

_____

Journal Instructions

Write in here as inspiration takes you. Give yourself the freedom to skip around, and no guilt for missing days, just happiness and joy from writing, creating and learning.

SOAP stands for Scripture, Observation, Application and Prayer. Use those pages for your devotional studies.

Colored pencils work best, but gel pens and markers are great pops of color. Build on the doodles and create your own zentangles.

Blessings upon you!

Things on my Mind...

S

O

A

P

Prayers on my Heart

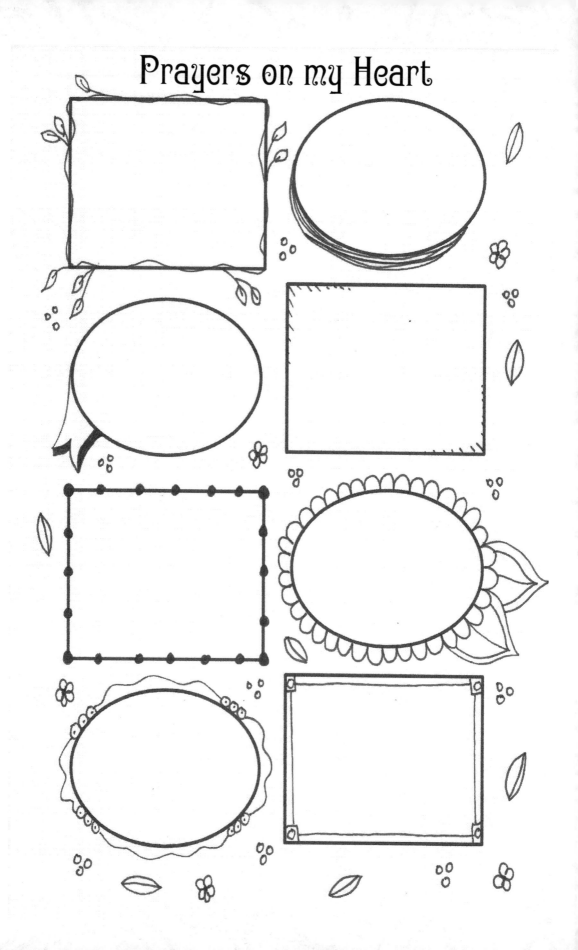

List love

Song in my Heart

Gratitude of my Heart

by
GRACE
you have been saved

Things on my Mind...

S

O

A

P

Prayers on my Heart

List love

Song in my Heart

Gratitude of my Heart

Things on my Mind...

S

O

A

P

Prayers on my Heart

Song in my Heart

List love

Gratitude of my Heart

Grace

given to me

Things on my Mind...

S

O

A

P

Prayers on my Heart

List love

Song in my Heart

Gratitude of my Heart

Speak the truth in love.

Things on my Mind...

S

O

A

P

Prayers on my Heart

List love

Song in my Heart

Gratitude of my Heart

Serve

wholeheartedly

Things on my Mind...

S

O

A

P

Prayers on my Heart

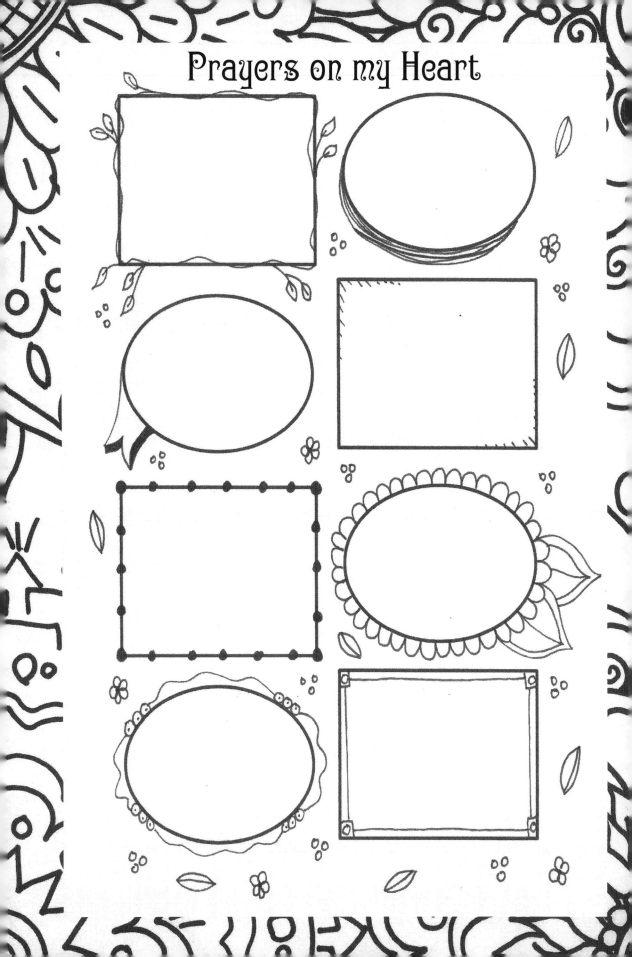

List love

Song in my Heart

ATTITUDE

is a reflection of your heart

Gratitude of my Heart

Things on my Mind...

S

O

A

P

Prayers on my Heart

Kindness

List love

Song in my Heart

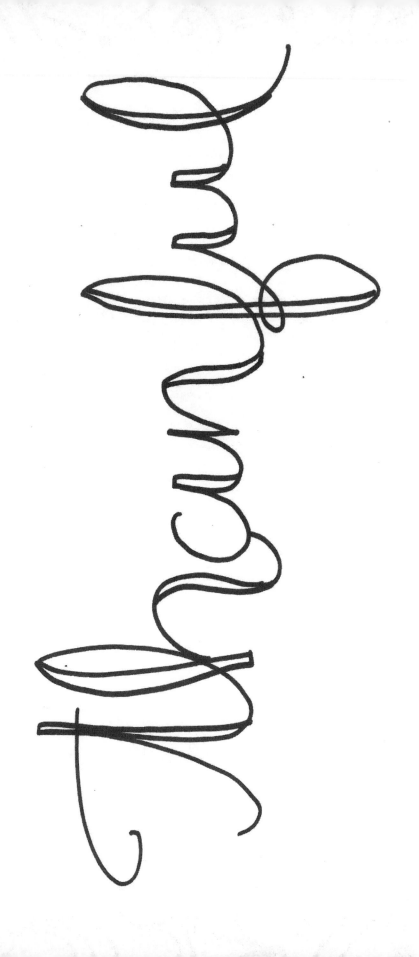

Gratitude of my Heart

grace
&
peace

Made in the USA
Middletown, DE
09 March 2018